MauindiArts

VOLUME ONE

TRANQUILITY

COLOURING BOOK

More at **www.etsy.com/au/shop/MauindiArts.** Find us on Facebook: **www.facebook.com/MauindiArts**

© MauindiArts 2015. Artwork by Maui Indi. Graphic Design by karenkluss.com

ISBN-13: 978 1 51500 282 6

Made in the USA
Columbia, SC
21 October 2021